Written by Bridget Ryan
Illustrated by Jason Carter

Story and illustrations inspired by trickster characters everywhere.

www.whoisboo.com

The continuing adventures of one trickster rabbit begins with Boo racing across the prairies...

...racing against his brother.

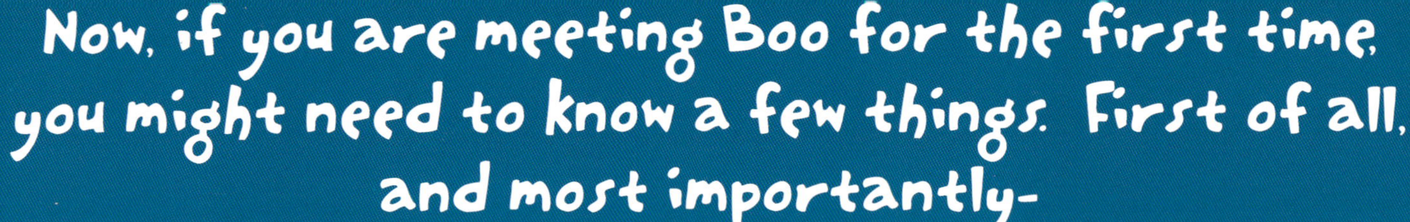

Now, if you are meeting Boo for the first time, you might need to know a few things. First of all, and most importantly-

this is Boo.

Boo is a rabbit who likes to play tricks.

Not mean tricks-

but helpful tricks!

Boo is not only curious,
he is helpful.

He is also in a very, very big hurry!

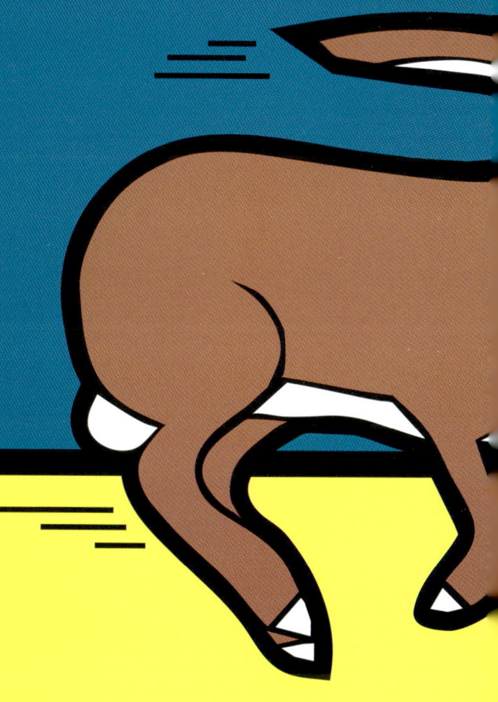

Boo is constantly in a race with his brother around the world. They keep racing around the world because frankly, they forgot where they put the finish line.

They race EVERYWHERE!

They race through the forest.

They race over The Rocky Mountains.

They race along The Great Wall of China...

...pausing briefly to take a photo!
It's the Great Wall of China for goodness sake!

They race over large bodies of water, jumping on and over islands, but that's no problem for them, being rabbits and all.

In Australia, Boo meets KANGAROO, who has just as much spring in her step as he does!

He stops for a quick 'hello!'

They leap over the Indian Ocean, and land squarely in the middle of the jungle.
How exciting! How hot! How humid!

Boo and his brother race through
rolling hills, lush green trees and the wet rainforest.

Boo carefully tip-toes past a grumpy GORILLA...

he high-fives a happy HIPPOPOTAMUS...

and has a good laugh with HYENA (although neither of them said anything particularly funny).

Boo stops for a quick breath when he discovers SPIDER MONKEY sitting at the base of a tree looking very upset.

'Hello friend' said Boo, 'why the long face? Why are you sitting at the bottom of this tree?'

'I am exhausted and hungry' said SPIDER MONKEY.
'I can't seem to hold myself up while I collect food which is at the top of this tree!

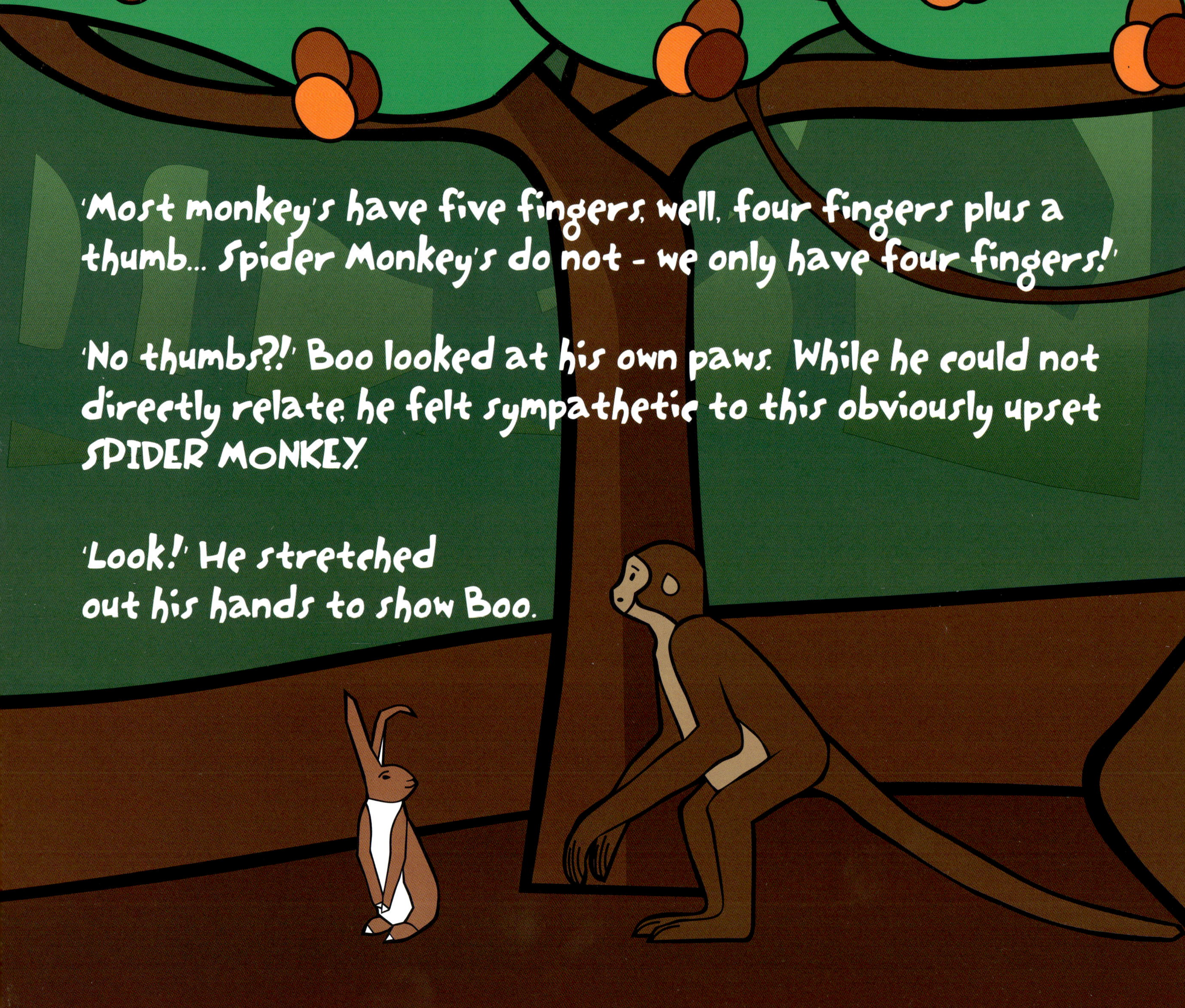
'Most monkey's have five fingers, well, four fingers plus a thumb... Spider Monkey's do not - we only have four fingers!'
'No thumbs?!' Boo looked at his own paws. While he could not directly relate, he felt sympathetic to this obviously upset SPIDER MONKEY.
'Look!' He stretched out his hands to show Boo.

'1, 2, 3, 4!' said SPIDER MONKEY. 'This makes it difficult for a monkey like me to climb and gather the fruits and vegetables to eat them! I find it hard to hold myself up. Watch!'

And with that, he jumped onto the tree.

Boo watched as he climbed with ease, but as soon as he let go to grab a piece of fruit, he started to slide down...
slide way down...
to the bottom of the tree!

"Hmmm" thought Boo. No question about it, SPIDER MONKEY was frustrated. Surely there was something he could do to help.

Remembering that one must consider all sides when thinking, Boo thought to the left.

Boo thought to the right.

He thought up,

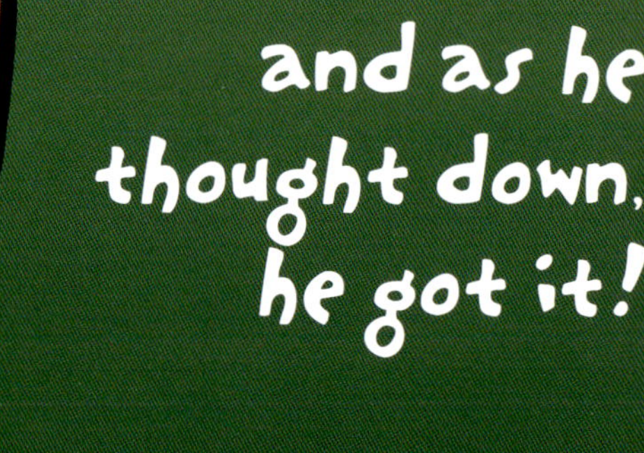

and as he thought down, he got it!

'Of course!' Boo blurted out.
'You only have four fingers because you are lucky enough to have five hands!'

'FIVE hands?!' SPIDER MONKEY was pretty sure he only saw four.

'Your fifth hand is your tail!' said Boo. 'Your tail is your strongest and sturdiest of hands. It will hold you steady while the other hands grab the food and eat!'

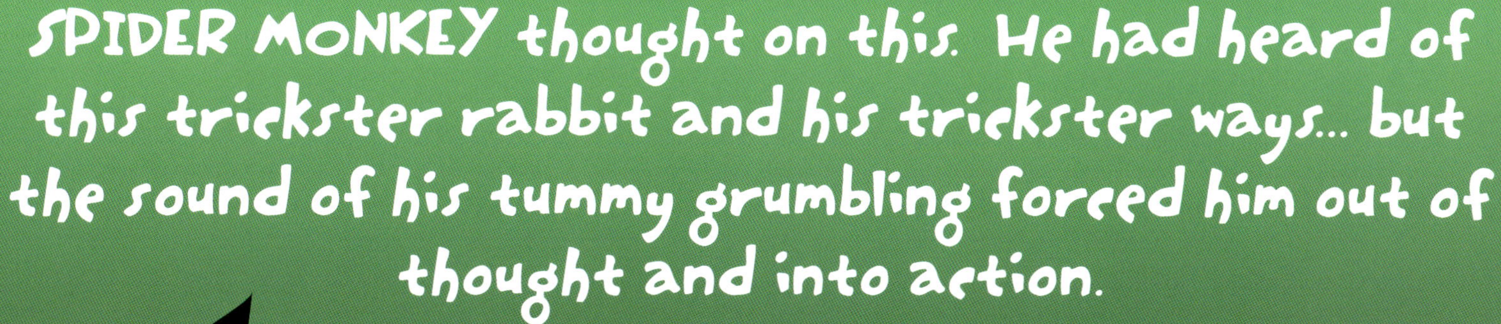

SPIDER MONKEY thought on this. He had heard of this trickster rabbit and his trickster ways... but the sound of his tummy grumbling forced him out of thought and into action.

'I'll try it' declared SPIDER MONKEY.

Up the tree
he went.

He climbed-

and he climbed-

and he climbed-
-and at the top of the tree he could feel his tail holding him rock steady. He happily began to feast!

'Delicious!' exclaimed SPIDER MONKEY, his mouth full of fruits. This was one time Boo didn't mind someone speaking with a mouth full!

'This is great! I can stay up here all day and eat and rest and then eat some more! Why I could even hang upside down!'
And so, as one would expect...

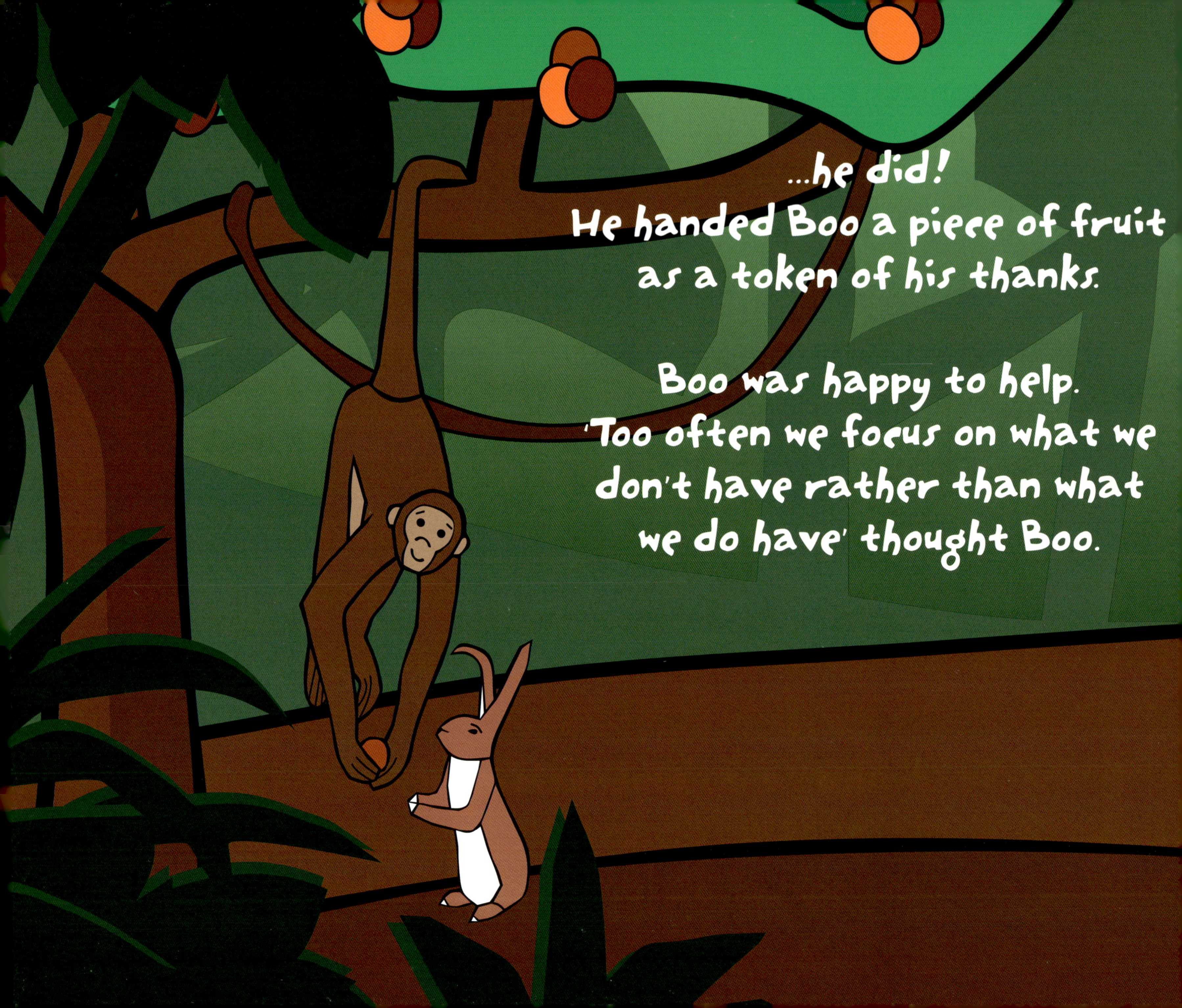

...he did!
He handed Boo a piece of fruit as a token of his thanks.

Boo was happy to help.
'Too often we focus on what we don't have rather than what we do have' thought Boo.

He was about to take a bite into the fruit when he heard the sounds of his brother's feet rustling through the jungle floor. Time to go!

He left SPIDER MONKEY happily swinging in the tree as he bolted out of the jungle...

...and into the ocean!

Boo quickly became fast friends with a HUMPBACK WHALE who offered him a ride. Boo thought it might be nice to give his legs a rest.

But just as they began cruising along-

-the HUMPBACK WHALE exhaled air and his top blew! Boo went flying into the air!

He flew over mountains...
over lakes...
and over valleys.

Boo landed back on the prairies, where he first started the race, now putting him well behind his brother. Luckily, he landed face-first into a small hole.

It was dark underground, but when his eyes adjusted, he saw that he was not alone!

PRAIRIE DOGS!

He was about to introduce himself when he felt a yank, a tug and a pull. Suddenly he was seeing sky again.

The smallest (and clearly the strongest) of prairie dogs had set him free in one swift move!

'Thank you, friend' said Boo.

Just then the PRAIRIE DOG darted behind him to hide.

'Hello?' said Boo

'Hello!' said PRAIRIE DOG briefly peeking out from his hiding spot.

It seemed to Boo that this was one very frightened PRAIRIE DOG.

'Storm is coming... Look!'

It was true! Boo saw big puffy storm clouds rolling in across the prairies. The wind picked up and he could hear thunder in the distance. PRAIRIE DOG couldn't stop shaking.

It was difficult for him when a storm loomed. He had so much work to do but he couldn't get over his feelings of being very nervous, very shaky and very scared.

And really, who could blame him? Storms can be scary
(especially if you don't like big sounds).

'I have to gather food to take to my family but I find that I am so frightened, I can't get anything done!'

Boo was all too familiar with feelings of being frightened. Just then, Boo pulled something out of his pocket.

(It should be noted that most rabbits do not have pockets, but Boo was a trickster rabbit in every way!)

It was MICHAEL!
His stuffy!
Boo often travelled with him and if he ever became nervous his stuffy made him feel a whole lot better.

Certainly PRAIRIE DOG could use something to hold onto that might make him feel better, but what?

A bale of hay seemed a little awkward...

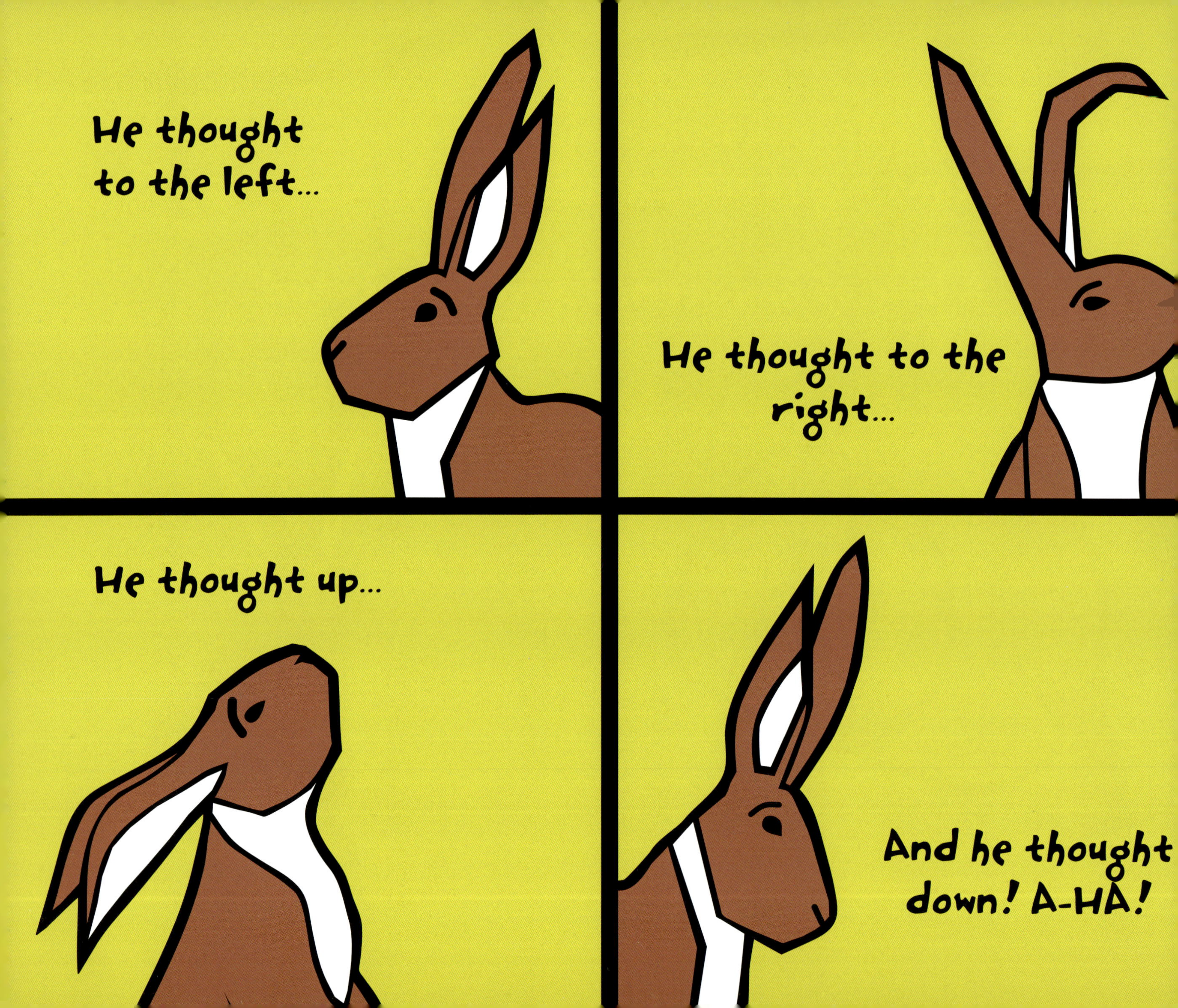
He thought to the left...
He thought to the right...
He thought up...
And he thought down! A-HA!

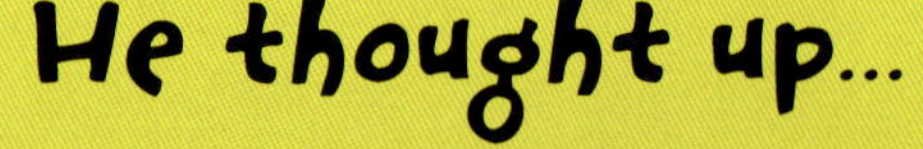

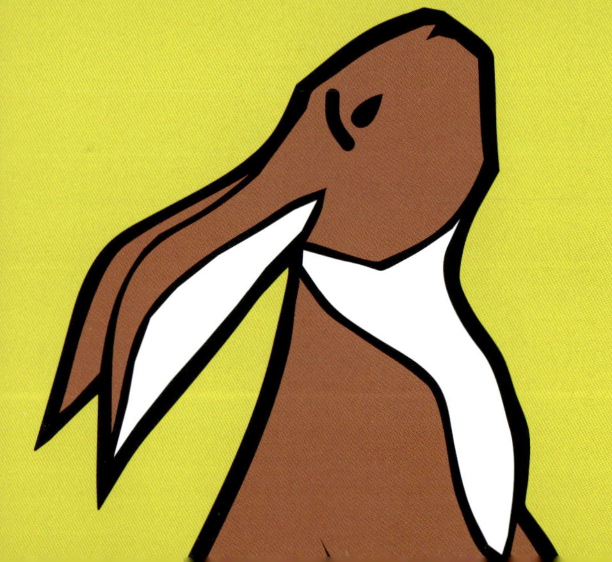

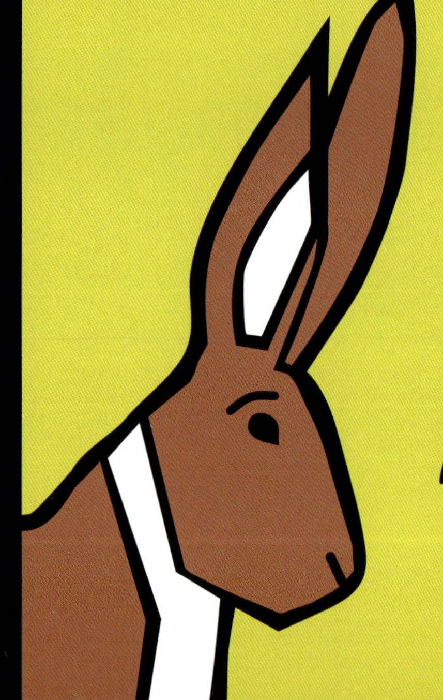

Boo picked up a stalk of wheat and handed it to PRAIRIE DOG.

'What's this for?' quivered PRAIRIE DOG.

Boo explained that it was a special piece of prairie grass and that when a storm loomed, it would take away all of his feelings of being afraid and make him feel a whole lot better. All he had to do was squeeze it with all his might! PRAIRIE DOG was doubtful.

Boo told him that in his travels around the world, he had come across many animals who had felt afraid once or twice...

The GIRAFFE, tall and noble-

has a rubber ducky!

An ELEPHANT, slow moving and elegant-

has a blankie!

And the LION, fierce and glorious...

has a bright red top!

PRAIRIE DOG was about to say something when a huge clap of thunder shook the ground. He grabbed onto his new stalk of wheat and squeezed with all his might!

Gradually, he felt better and better!

The storm passed and it was time for PRAIRIE DOG to get back to work. But before he left...

'Thank you, friend' said PRAIRIE DOG.
And then he was on his way.

Boo knew it was time to get moving as well!

Boo had much ground to cover if he wanted to catch up to his brother. Eyes forward, Boo raced along wondering just HOW far behind he was and WHO he would meet next?